Bilingual Edition

READING POWER

Edición Bilingüe

Venus Williams

Tennis Champion

Campeona del tenis

Heather Feldman

Traducción al español
Mauricio Velázquez de León

The Rosen Publishing Group's
PowerKids Press™ & **Buenas Letras**™
New York

For Sophie Megan
Para Sophie Megan

Published in 2002 by The Rosen Publishing Group, Inc.
29 East 21st Street, New York, NY 10010

First Bilingual Edition 2002
First Edition in English 2001

Book Design: Michael de Guzman

Photo Credits: pp. 5, 15, 17, 19 © CLIVE BRUNSKILL/ALLSPORT; p. 7 © KEN LEVINE/ALLSPORT; p. 9 © JACK ATLEY/ALLSPORT; p. 11 © AL BELLO/ALLSPORT; pp. 13, 21 © GARY M. PRIOR/ALLSPORT.

Feldman, Heather.
    Venus Williams : tennis champion = Venus Williams : campeona del tenis /
Feldman, Heather : traducción al español Mauricio Velázquez de León.
        p. cm.— (Reading power)
    Includes index.
    Summary: A biography of the young tennis player who has been ranked among the top ten women players in the world.
    ISBN 0-8239-6138-9 (alk. paper)
    1. Williams, Venus, 1980- —Juvenile literature. 2. Tennis players—United States—Biography—Juvenile literature. 3. Afro-American women tennis players—Biography—Juvenile literature. [1. Williams, Venus, 1980- 2. Tennis players. 3. Afro-Americans—Biography. 4. Women—Biography. 5. Spanish language materials— Bilingual.]
    I. Title. II. Series.

GV994.W49 F45 2001
796.342'092—dc21
[B]

Word Count:
English: 118
Spanish: 113

Manufactured in the United States of America

Contents

Contenido

Venus Williams plays tennis.

———————

Venus Williams es tenista profesional.

Venus has played tennis for many years. She has played since she was a young girl.

———————

Venus ha jugado al tenis durante muchos años. Ha jugado desde que era niña.

Venus has a sister named
Serena. Serena plays
tennis, too.

———————

Venus tiene una
hermana llamada Serena.
Ella también es tenista.

Venus and Serena win prizes. They are both great tennis players. They are great friends, too.

Venus y Serena ganan trofeos.
Las dos son muy buenas
jugadoras y
buenas
amigas.

11

Venus can move fast. She
moves fast to
get to the ball.

Venus puede
moverse muy rápido para
alcanzar la pelota.

Venus can jump high. She jumps high to hit the ball.

———

Venus puede saltar muy alto y golpear la pelota en el aire.

15

Venus likes to wear her hair in beads. Venus has a lot of style.

————

A Venus le gusta usar cuentas en el cabello. Venus tiene un estilo muy personal.

Venus uses a big racket.
She uses the racket to hit
the tennis ball hard.

———

Venus usa una raqueta
muy grande. Con ella
puede golpear la pelota
con fuerza.

Venus is happy when she wins a prize. She wins prizes for playing tennis. Venus is a great tennis player.

Cuando Venus gana se pone muy contenta. Gana trofeos jugando al tenis. Venus es una gran tenista.

21

Glossary

prizes (PRYZ-iz) What a person sometimes gets when he or she wins games.

racket (RAK-it) The object a tennis player holds and uses to hit the tennis ball.

style (STYL) A special way of acting or looking that makes a person who he or she is.

tennis (TEN-is) A sport where two or four people hit a ball back and forth over a net using tennis rackets.

Glosario

estilo Forma especial de verse o actuar que define a una persona.

raqueta (la) Objeto que usan los tenistas para golpear la pelota de tenis.

tenis Deporte en el que dos o cuatro personas golpean una pelota por encima de una red usando raquetas.

trofeo (el) Lo que obtiene un deportista cuando gana un campeonato.

Here is another good book to read about Venus Williams:

Para leer más acerca de Venus Williams, te recomendamos este libro:

Venus Williams (Galaxy of Superstars)
By Virginia Aronson
Chelsea House Publishers

To learn more about tennis, check out these Web sites:

Para aprender más sobre tenis, visita estas páginas de Internet:

http://www.yahooligans.com/Sports_
   and_Recreation/Tennis
http://www.excite.com/sports/tennis/

Index

Índice